Dates of a Decade

THE 1970s

Nathaniel Harris

with additional text by Jacqueline Laks Gorman

ARCTURUS

This edition first published by Arcturus Publishing
Distributed by Black Rabbit Books
123 South Broad Street
Mankato
Minnesota MN 56001

Copyright © 2009 Arcturus Publishing Limited

Printed in the United States

All rights reserved

Series concept: Alex Woolf
Editor and picture researcher: Alex Woolf
U.S. editor: Jacqueline Laks Gorman
Designer: Phipps Design

Library of Congress Cataloging-in-Publication Data

Harris, Nathaniel, 1937-
 The 1970s / Nathaniel Harris.
   p. cm. -- (Dates of a decade)
 Includes index.
 ISBN 978-1-84837-283-2 (hardcover)
 1. History, Modern--1945-1989--Juvenile literature. I. Title.

 D848.H385 2010
 909.82'7--dc22

                    2009000007

Picture credits:
Corbis: 4 (Bettmann), 5 (Bettmann), 6 (Bettmann), 7 (Bettmann), 9, 14 (Bettmann),
16 (Hulton-Deutsch Collection), 18 (Jose Fuste Raga), 20 (Bettmann), 21
(Bettmann), 24 (Bettmann), 25 (Chris Rainier), 28 (Bettmann), 29 (Mike
Segar/Reuters), cover right and 33 (Bettmann), 34 (Vittoriano Rastelli), cover cen-
tre and 35 (Bettmann), cover left and 36 (Bettmann), 37 (Bettmann), 38
(Bettmann), 43 (Matthew Cavanaugh/epa), 44 (Bettmann).
Getty Images: 10, 11 (Popperfoto), 12 (AFP), 13 (AFP), 15, 17 (Popperfoto), 22, 23
(AFP), 26, 27, 39 (AFP), 40 (Time & Life Pictures), 41 (Howard Ruffner/Time & Life
Pictures), 42 (Cynthia Johnson/Time & Life Pictures), 45 (Dirck Halstead/Time &
Life Pictures).
Science Photo Library: 30 (NASA), 31 (NASA).
Shutterstock: 19 (Jan Kranendonk).

Contents

GLOBAL EVENTS

UNITED STATES EVENTS

Three Hijacked Airliners Are Blown Up

The explosions were set off in Dawson's Field, a disused airstrip in the Jordanian Desert. The planes belonged to British, American, and Swiss airlines. They had been hijacked by Palestinian terrorists, who destroyed them when they believed a rescue attempt was starting. They removed the passengers and released most of them. But the fleeing terrorists took more than 50 passengers with them and held them as hostages. It seemed likely that they would be killed unless the Palestinians' demands were met.

The first of the three hijacked airliners explodes at Dawson's Field in the Jordanian Desert. After the destruction of the other two, the terrorists left the scene with their hostages.

Deal or No Deal?

Some governments decided to do a deal. Britain, West Germany, and Switzerland released several imprisoned terrorists, and in return the hostages from their countries were freed. On one level the deal was a success. But it highlighted the difficult issue of how governments should respond to hijackings and hostage-taking. If they gave way to the terrorists' demands, the terrorists won and would be encouraged to continue. Refusing to negotiate would frustrate and eventually discourage them. However, such a tough attitude risked the lives of innocent hostages, and few governments felt able to act entirely consistently.

Decade of terrorism

Such issues mattered, because terrorism became a worldwide problem in the 1970s. The Palestinians, in their struggle against Israel, targeted individuals and countries they regarded as their enemy's supporters. Conflict in Northern Ireland spread to mainland Britain when the IRA (Irish Republican Army) started a bombing campaign there. Other violent groups included the Angry Brigade (Britain), the Baader-Meinhof gang (West Germany), the Red Brigades (Italy), the Weathermen (United States), the Japanese Red Army, and the Tupumaros (Uruguay).

Ongoing struggle

The 1972 killing of Israeli athletes at the Munich Olympics and the kidnapping and murder of the Italian statesman Aldo Moro (1978) were among the many terrorist outrages of the 1970s. Terrorism became international as groups with different aims sometimes worked together. For example, in 1975 the notorious revolutionary "Carlos the Jackal" (Illich Ramirez Sanchez) helped the Palestinians by taking the ministers of the Arab oil states as hostages. However, the terrorists also suffered defeats. The Baader-Meinhof gang were captured in 1972, and in 1976 the Israelis staged a daring attack on a hijacked plane at Entebbe in Uganda, rescuing the hostages and killing the hijackers. But by the end of the 1970s, the struggle against terrorism was far from won.

Aldo Moro, a former Italian prime minister, is shown in a photo taken by the Red Brigades terrorists, who kidnapped him in 1978. Moro appears with the Red Brigades' flag in the background. The Italian government refused to accept the terrorists' demands, and Moro was murdered.

◉ eye witness

At two-thirty in the morning, I was awakened…. They wanted me up front, for questioning…. I went and was told to sign a piece of paper … but I couldn't sign because my hand was shaking. They told us to get off the plane … not knowing where I was going, not knowing when I would see my family again … I was sure I was going to be killed…. We were put on board a bus. It was myself and nine other people…. Two guerrillas sat up front carrying machine guns facing us – as if we were going to run somewhere.

David Raab (a 17-year-old hostage in 1970),
Terror in Black September (Palgrave Macmillan, 2007)

- **SEE ALSO**
  Pages 10–11: September 5, 1972
  Murder at the Munich Olympics

  Pages 14–15: October 6, 1973
  Egypt and Syria Attack Israel

- **FURTHER INFORMATION**
  📖 Books:
  Terrorism by Alex Woolf (Wayland, 2003)
  🖱 Websites:
  www.bbc.co.uk/history/recent/sept_11/changing_faces_01.shtml
  A handy seven-page BBC history and discussion of terrorism

Bangladesh Is Born

On December 16, 1971, India emerged victorious from a two-week conflict with Pakistan. In the eastern sector of the war, the Pakistani commander, General Niazi, and his entire army surrendered unconditionally. The ceremony was held in public at Dhaka, the capital of what had been East Pakistan (also known as East Bengal). India's victory ensured that East Pakistan's struggle for independence succeeded, and the former province became the new nation of Bangladesh.

Two Pakistans

Britain had ruled the Indian subcontinent until 1947, when it was divided into two newly independent states, India and Pakistan. Pakistan consisted of two geographically distinct regions. West Pakistan and East Pakistan were separated by 995 miles (1,600 kilometres) of Indian territory, and the Bengali-speaking people in the eastern province were different in character and traditions from those in the west. The centers of government and power were located in West Pakistan, so the east, despite its larger population, was neglected. Resentment built up until December 1970, when elections were held throughout Pakistan. All the East Pakistan seats were won by the Awami League, which demanded autonomy (self-rule) for the province.

Three children from a Bangladeshi border village, newly arrived at a refugee camp. Huge numbers of people fled to India when the Pakistan army brutally suppressed the independence movement.

What the papers said

It was a day of many dramatic happenings. First there was no response until the eleventh hour from the Pakistan military command in the East to the call for surrender.... Finally came the surrender to Lieutenant-General J. S. Aurora, commander of the Indian forces and the Mukti Bahini (the Bangla Desh fighters) in the East, who flew by helicopter to Dacca.... Mrs. Gandhi, the Indian Prime Minister, who broke the news to Parliament ... was given a hero's ovation such as has never been seen in the two Houses before.

Kulddip Nayar, *The Times*, December 16, 1971

Scene of triumph: smiling Indian Brigadier General Misra leads his troops into Dhaka, the capital of East Pakistan. After the fall of the city, Pakistan was forced to agree to a ceasefire, and the war ended in India's favor. As a result, East Pakistan became an independent country under its new name, Bangladesh.

A revolt crushed

The Pakistani government was reluctant to accept the result, and people in East Pakistan began to talk of independence. But the government struck first. In March 1971, martial law was imposed and the Awami leader, Sheikh Mujibur Rahman, was arrested – but not before he made a radio broadcast proclaiming an independent East Pakistan, now renamed Bangladesh. Bengali units of the Pakistani army rallied to the new state, but troops from the west were airlifted in and crushed the revolt. The savage behavior of the Pakistani forces led to thousands of deaths, and millions of Bangladeshis fled to neighboring India.

War and independence

Relations between India and Pakistan had often been strained, and they grew worse when India began to help Bangladeshi guerrillas. In December, war broke out between India and Pakistan. Fierce struggles in the west ended in stalemate. But, unexpectedly, the Indian army advanced rapidly in the east with the help of Bangladeshi guerrillas and won a swift victory. Bangladesh had won its independence, and Sheikh Mujibur Rahman became its first prime minister. However, the new country found it hard to achieve stability, and a long period of violence and uncertainty followed a coup that overthrew Rahman in 1975.

- **SEE ALSO**

  Pages 24–25: April 29, 1975
  Saigon Falls to the North Vietnamese

  Pages 36–37: February 1, 1979
  Ayatollah Khomeini Returns to Iran

- **FURTHER INFORMATION**

  📖 Books:
  Bangladesh by David Cumming
  (Macdonald, 1999)

  🖰 Websites:
  www.virtualbangladesh.com/history/
  A good multimedia site, told from an intensely patriotic angle

Murder at the Munich Olympics

The 1972 Olympic Games were held in Munich in southern Germany. As usual, competitors were housed in their own Olympic Village, and because of terrorist threats the Village was heavily policed. But on the night of September 5, toward the end of the Games, five men, dressed like athletes in track suits, managed to climb into the Israeli compound. They made contact with three others who had bluffed their way in with false documents. The men all belonged to Black September, a Palestinian terrorist group.

A Black September terrorist stands defiantly on the balcony of the Israeli team's quarters in the Olympic village. The terrorists have seized hostages and are making their demands known.

Armed with submachine guns, the terrorists attacked the building that housed the Israelis. A wrestling coach was shot down and a weightlifter died helping fellow athletes to escape. The terrorists captured nine Israeli athletes and held them as hostages, threatening to kill them if security forces attacked. The terrorists stated their demands: the release of hundreds of jailed Palestinians and other prisoners, including two convicted German terrorists. The West German government appeared to give way. The gang and its hostages were taken by helicopter to an airport to be flown to Egypt.

Failed rescue

In reality, the West Germans had prepared a trap. As the terrorists and their hostages crossed the tarmac to board the waiting plane, the airport lights were turned out. Police sharpshooters were in position and ready to pick off the Palestinians. But they failed to kill them all and there was a gun battle. At its end, four of

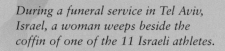

the terrorists had been killed and three had been captured; only one managed to escape. All nine of the Israeli hostages were dead. Black September had not won, but the rescue attempt had failed disastrously.

Palestinians and Israelis

The attack on the Israeli compound was a shocking episode in a long and painful conflict. The founding of the Jewish state of Israel in 1948 and Israel's victories over Arab states left millions of Palestinians as refugees or living under Israeli occupation. The Palestinians founded guerrilla and terrorist organizations, most of them grouped together as the PLO (Palestine Liberation Organization), to attack Israel. By also committing terrorist acts in other countries, the Palestinians hoped to publicize their plight while hurting Israel and its supporters. The policy brought some successes, but in the long run generated anger rather than sympathy. Finally, in 1988, the PLO publicly gave up terrorism, though progress on the Palestinian-Israeli issue remained limited.

During a funeral service in Tel Aviv, Israel, a woman weeps beside the coffin of one of the 11 Israeli athletes.

What the papers said

As they [the terrorists] tried to rush the Israelis, they were halted at the door by a coach.... Tuvia Sokolsky ... said ... "I heard this shout: 'Boys, get out!' I saw a strange picture – one of the men on the team ... using all his strength to keep the door closed.... I think he saved my life. Because of the warning, I was able to escape from the room." Gus Psabari, a wrestler, dashed out in a hail of bullets.... "I think I ran faster than [Olympic sprinter] Valery Borzov; I think I broke the record for the dash."

David Binder in the *New York Times*, September 6, 1972

- **SEE ALSO**
  Pages 4–5: September 12, 1970
  Three Hijacked Airliners Are Blown Up

- **FURTHER INFORMATION**
  📖 Books:
  The Munich Olympics by Hal Marcovitz (Chelsea House, 2002)
  🖱 Websites:
  www.time.com/time/magazine/article/
  0,9171,906384,00.html?internalid=ACA
  A full account from *Time*

Chile's Government Is Overthrown

Trouble started at 6 A.M., when Chilean naval units occupied the port of Valparaiso. The defense minister, Orlando Letellier, informed the president, Salvador Allende. Then Letellier went to his ministry in the Chilean capital, Santiago. Military men were waiting for him, and he was immediately arrested. A radio broadcast announced the formation of a new government, drawn from the chiefs of the armed forces. But Allende refused to resign and leave the country. At about 9 A.M., he made a broadcast on the only radio station not in rebel hands. Though defiant, he made it clear that he was expecting to die.

The palace besieged

Soon afterward, military units and Sherman tanks surrounded the presidential palace and bombarded it. Loyal guards and policemen fought back with bazookas and machine guns, although the enemy's superior numbers were bound to triumph. After a brief truce, during which the women in the palace were allowed to leave, jets struck with rockets and bombs. The two-hour siege ended when soldiers stormed the blazing building. Allende was found dead, having apparently killed himself rather than be captured. The new military regime, headed by General Augusto Pinochet, dealt savagely with Allende's supporters. A 17-year dictatorship followed, creating deep divisions between Chileans that continued into the 21st century.

The La Moneda presidential palace under siege. Rebel Chilean troops fire down on the palace from a rooftop during the coup that overthrew Chile's elected president, Salvador Allende, on September 11, 1973. Allende himself died in the attack.

Latin America

Allende died because his government's policies threatened powerful interests. His Socialist Party was pledged to nationalize (transfer from private to government control) important interests and improve the lives of the poor. The government's enemies included the rich and powerful, and also the United States, whose Central Intelligence Agency (CIA) was involved in planning and funding the coup. Allende's overthrow was striking because his government had been democratically elected in 1970 and again in 1973.

In Chile, as in most of Latin America, political stability was hard to achieve. The gulf between rich and poor was very wide, and reforms that might lessen the power and privileges of the rich were fiercely resisted. The dominant regional power, the United States, was determined to defend American business interests in the region. The United States was also suspicious of radical and socialist movements, fearing that if they gained power they would become allies of the Soviet Union, as Cuba had done. U.S. interventions in Latin American countries, either openly or secretly, continued into the 1980s.

General Augusto Pinochet (left) with Chilean President Salvador Allende. In August 1973, Allende appointed Pinochet head of the armed forces. Three weeks later, Pinochet launched the coup that overthrew him.

⦿ eye witness

The following eye witness account of the scene in Santiago reached Buenos Aires after the reporter, Agustin Giannoni, had been held for hours at gunpoint by rebel soldiers: "We have now spent 14 hours in our semi-destroyed office in ... Santiago – windows broken, no telephone, no water, no food. In the neighboring office ... women – two of them wounded – crying and screaming hysterically. Others weep silently. The streets are empty except for military patrols. The predominant sound is machine-gun fire. The only news we have tells of hundreds dead, but the most recent report speaks of 4,500.... Everyone now is scared stiff."

Guardian, September 14, 1973

- **SEE ALSO**
  Pages 24–25: April 29, 1975
  Saigon Falls to the North Vietnamese
  Pages 38–39: December 24, 1979
  Soviet Forces Enter Afghanistan

- **FURTHER INFORMATION**
  📖 Books:
  Chile by Marion Morrison (Evans, 2005)
  🖱 Websites:
  www.mundoandino.com/Chile/History-1973-coup
  The 1973 coup and Chile in the later 1970s

Egypt and Syria Attack Israel

Early in the afternoon, Syrian planes attacked Israeli positions on the Golan Heights, Syrian territory held by Israel since 1967. A few minutes later, 250 miles (400 kilometres) to the west, Egyptian commandos launched an assault across the Suez Canal against Israel's fortified Bar-Lev line on the east bank. October 6 was a day when Jews fasted and did not travel – Yom Kippur, which gave its name to the war that followed.

Yom Kippur War

The coordinated Syrian-Egyptian offensives took the Israelis by surprise. The Golan and Suez were only lightly defended, since most of Israel's army were reservists – trained men and women who led ordinary civilian lives unless they were called up during a war. During the first few days of the Yom Kippur War, Israel was in peril while it struggled to mobilize its forces. Syrian tanks drove the Israelis back across the Golan. The Egyptians broke through the Bar-Lev line, and Israel's air force suffered heavy casualties in its attempts to stem their advance.

Holding on

For two days, the fate of Israel hung in the balance. In the most vulnerable sector, the Golan, Israeli tanks just held on until reinforcements arrived and the Syrians were forced to retreat. The main Israeli effort was then

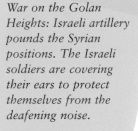

War on the Golan Heights: Israeli artillery pounds the Syrian positions. The Israeli soldiers are covering their ears to protect themselves from the deafening noise.

directed against the Egyptians. On October 15, in a daring move, Israeli units landed on the west bank of the Suez Canal and cut off the Egyptian army in Sinai. By the 26th, when a United Nations ceasefire came into force, the Egyptian Third Army was encircled and Israeli tanks were within 40 miles (65 kilometres) of the Syrian capital, Damascus.

Road to peace

Israel had won, though at a heavy cost. However, the war had an even greater impact on Egypt, which had fought well enough to banish the memory of earlier defeats. This may have made it easier for Egypt's president, Anwar Sadat, to follow a bold new policy. He ended Egypt's close relationship with the Soviet Union and sought aid and friendship from the United States. Even more boldly, he began talks with Israel that culminated in the 1979 Camp David agreement. Under its terms, Egypt recovered the vast area of Sinai it had lost in the 1967 war and made peace with Israel. This seemed like a major breakthrough. However, there was no peace between Israel and other Arab states. The Middle East remained a dangerously tense region.

Discussion in the desert: Israeli generals Ariel Sharon (right) and Haim Bar-Lev consult the map, shortly after the Israeli landings on the west bank of the Suez Canal that turned the Yom Kippur War against Egypt.

● eye witness

That Yom Kippur morning ... three Phantoms flying north ... evoked some astonishment. Those planes were just about the only machines in motion ... anywhere in Israel.... At 2 in the afternoon ... I noticed to my amazement clusters of people huddled round transistor radios as well as a sudden movement of traffic.... Taxis were handing out mobilization orders. I saw several men receive them on the street ... they went back into their homes, reappearing ... in their army uniforms and carrying their guns. With a hasty farewell to their families, they were on their way to ... their units at the front.

Theodore Friedman, quoted in L. Soshak and A. L. Eisenberg, *Momentous Century* (Cornwall Books, 1984)

- **SEE ALSO**
  Pages 4–5: September 12, 1970
  Three Hijacked Airlines Are Blown Up

- **FURTHER INFORMATION**
  📖 Books:
  Israel and the Arab States in Conflict by Nathaniel Harris (Wayland, 1998)
  Websites:
  news.bbc.co.uk/aboutbbcnews/hi/news_update/newsid_3853000/3853345.stm
  Inside Egypt with Israeli troops; plus interesting information about how wars were reported in 1973

17 OCTOBER 1973

The Price of Oil Soars

Sheikh Ahmed Zaki Yamani made a statement on October 17 that had worldwide consequences. Yamani was the head of OPEC, an organization that brought together the world's major oil-exporting countries. OPEC was dominated by Saudi Arabia and other Arab states, although it also included non-Arab countries such as Iran, Nigeria, and Venezuela. Yamani announced the previous day's decision – to raise the price of OPEC's oil dramatically, from $3.00 to $5.12 a barrel.

● eye witness

Two very separate issues were at stake. One had political implications. That was the war and the question of oil as a political instrument.... The other was the price of oil.... I realized the political and economic impact of the date [of the OPEC decision] as soon as it happened.... For the first time the producers faced the consumers of the industrialized countries without anyone in the middle. October 16 was the demarcation. It was the day that OPEC seized power. Real power.

Sheikh Yamani, quoted in Jeffrey Robinson, *Yamani: The Inside Story* (Simon & Schuster, 1988)

The oil-rich states would now earn much more money. But the Arab producers also had a political motive, prompted by the Yom Kippur War. To punish states that they saw as supporters of Israel, oil production was to be reduced, and an embargo cut off supplies to the United States and the Netherlands. New cutbacks and price increases were introduced before the end of 1973, when crude (unprocessed) oil sold at almost four times the price it had been a few years earlier.

Panic reactions

Oil was vital to the running of advanced economies such as those of North America, Western Europe, and Japan. Supplied via Western-based oil companies, these economies had enjoyed

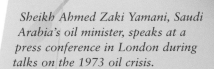

Sheikh Ahmed Zaki Yamani, Saudi Arabia's oil minister, speaks at a press conference in London during talks on the 1973 oil crisis.

In Britain, as in other countries, the oil crisis caused panic buying of gas. Long lines at gas stations like this one were a common sight.

decades of cheap fuel. Now, for the first time, the oil producers were not negotiating, but naming their price. The increases caused genuine shortages and also panic reactions. Vehicles formed long lines at gas pumps, despite soaring prices. In the United States, speed limits were imposed to reduce consumption. The high price of oil increased some countries' dependence on other fuels. In Britain, after British coal miners went on strike, the fuel shortage was so severe that a three-day working week was introduced in January 1974.

Long-term effects

In time, the advanced economies adjusted to higher fuel prices. The embargo against the Netherlands and the United States ended in November 1973 and March 1974, respectively. The Arabs' use of oil as a political weapon had only limited success, exerting some influence on Western European and Japanese attitudes. However, the crisis had serious long-term effects. A worldwide depression was avoided. But in many countries, inflation (rising general price levels) and unemployment became a problem, and it became harder to export enough to pay for expensive fuel imports. Vast wealth flowed into the oil states. Elsewhere, governments encouraged a search for alternative energy sources, such as North Sea oil and gas. For the first time, energy had become a major concern of political policy.

- **SEE ALSO**
  Pages 14–15: October 6, 1973
  Egypt and Syria Attack Israel

- **FURTHER INFORMATION**
  Books:
  Oil by John Farndon (Dorling Kindersley, 2007)
  Websites:
  www.opec.org/aboutus/history/history.htm
  A brief history of OPEC

20
OCTOBER
1973

Sydney Opera House Opens

It was a great moment for Australians. Masses of balloons were released. Australian air force planes flew overhead. People around Sydney Harbor cheered, and hundreds of boats sounded their horns. Queen Elizabeth II, as sovereign of Australia, had just declared Sydney Opera House open. Later in the day, Beethoven's Ninth Symphony became the first work performed in the building.

A controversial project

The opening marked the triumphant end to a long-running and controversial project. It began in 1956 with a competition for the best design for a proposed new opera house. The site chosen was spectacular – Bennelong Point, a narrow strip of land thrusting into the harbor. The winner of the competition was an almost unknown young Danish architect, Jørn Utzon, whose design broke with the dominant box-like "modernist" style of architecture. Instead, the opera house was to cover the entire point and to culminate in a series of shell roofs. From some angles it looked like a boat with huge sails, about to launch into the harbor. However, work on the opera house was painfully slow. Years passed and costs soared. Arguments flared, and Utzon resigned from the project in 1966. But when the building was completed, Australians were proud of it and its image became a symbol of Sydney and Australia.

Sydney Opera House, with its multiple shell roofs and spectacular harbour setting, is recognized as one of the great 20th-century buildings.

The Twin Towers

Other striking buildings were completed in the 1970s. New York's World Trade Center, the "Twin Towers," was designed by the American architect Minoru Yamasaki with brilliant light-reflecting aluminium sheathing on the outside. The Center was not a single building but consisted of two identical 110-story towers, at the time the tallest structures on earth. Their position on the skyline made them a symbol of New York until they were tragically destroyed by terrorists in 2001.

The Beaubourg

The Pompidou Center, or Beaubourg, in Paris was designed by British architect Richard Rogers and his Italian partner Renzo Piano. It was a center for the arts with a large open piazza (forecourt) where people could relax or perform. The outside was lined with features normally hidden inside – huge pipes, funnels, and fuse boxes supplying the water, electricity, and air conditioning, all painted in bright colors. Also on the outside, a transparent-sided escalator zigzagged to the top floor. At first regarded as bizarre, designs of this kind were to become increasingly common in modern architecture.

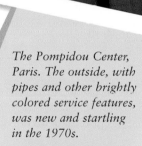

The Pompidou Center, Paris. The outside, with pipes and other brightly colored service features, was new and startling in the 1970s.

What the papers said

This was the grand leap of the imagination that Australia badly needed but had not yet made. Some older and more conservative local architects objected to the design as fanciful. And in between, through a barrage of publicity and cross-argument such as no building had ever received from the Australian press ... it became ... a cult object of enthusiasm, dissent, jokes and hobnailed political infighting.... Still, there it is, ... ready now for its ceremonial visit by Queen Elizabeth II – an Opera House that marks a watershed in Australian cultural history.

Australian art critic Robert Hughes in Time, October 8, 1973

- **FURTHER INFORMATION**
- 📖 **Books:**
  Sydney Opera House by Peggy J. Parks (Blackbirch, 2004)
- 🖰 **Websites:**
  architecture.about.com/library/blsydneyopera.htm
  A brief history and photo tour of the building

Nixon Announces His Resignation

At 9 P.M., 61-year-old President Richard M. Nixon spoke to the American people on television and radio. He told them that he intended to resign at noon the following day. Nixon became the first and only U.S. president to resign his office. He claimed that he was going because he no longer had enough support in Congress (the body that makes U.S. laws) to govern effectively. But most observers believed the real reason was Nixon's fear of impeachment – of being put on trial in Congress for trying to cover up the long-running Watergate scandal.

Illegal activities

Nixon's up-and-down political career peaked when he was finally elected president in 1968 and enjoyed some striking successes. He ended the long and painful U.S. involvement in Vietnam and greatly improved relations with communist China and the Soviet Union. In November 1972, Nixon won a landslide victory and a second four-year term as president. However, the event that would ruin him had already taken place.

Richard Nixon tells the nation that he intends to resign as U.S. president. He enjoyed considerable success until he was brought down by the Watergate scandal.

What the papers said

A President of the United States has resigned from office. It is a profoundly sad and profoundly heartening occasion. The sadness all but speaks for itself. Richard Nixon, a man whose entire adult professional life was dedicated to the quest for and exercise of the powers of the office of the presidency, leaves that office under a cloud of wrongdoing and shame.... [It is heartening because] it required the courage and ultimate decency and good sense of many ... in public life to reaffirm those standards of public conduct against which he was judged and found wanting.
Washington Post, August 9, 1974

Bob Woodward (left) and Carl Bernstein, writers for the Washington Post *newspaper. Their investigations and reporting did much to expose the Watergate scandal.*

On June 17, 1972, five burglars were caught trying to bug the offices of the opposition Democratic Party in the Watergate building in Washington, D.C. It gradually became clear that "Watergate" had been part of an illegal campaign to spy on and discredit people opposed to Nixon's reelection. More and more links emerged between the burglars and the White House. In April 1973, top presidential advisers and government members were forced to resign and later went to prison.

Tell-tale tapes

Nixon protested that he had not known about the illegalities. But he refused to hand over tapes on which his conversations and phone calls were recorded. And when the special prosecutor Archibald Cox demanded the tapes, Nixon dismissed him. The president wielded great power, but journalists, members of Congress and lawyers doggedly sought to discover the truth. When the U.S. Supreme Court forced Nixon to hand over the tapes, they showed that he knew a good deal about attempts to cover up the crime. The taped conversations also showed an ugly side to Nixon, including an almost insane hatred of journalists and "enemies," which helped to turn public feeling against him. After the first steps were taken toward impeachment, the president struggled on for a time before he finally gave up. He was succeeded by his vice president, Gerald Ford, who later pardoned Nixon, effectively closing the disastrous Watergate affair.

• **SEE ALSO**
Pages 8–9: February 21, 1972
President Nixon Visits China

• **FURTHER INFORMATION**
📖 Books:
The Watergate Scandal by Dan Elish (Scholastic, 2004)
🖱 Websites:
www.washingtonpost.com/wp-srv/politics/special/watergate/index.html
The Watergate Story. Full information and pictures from the *Washington Post* newspaper, which was prominent in investigating the cover-up.

Ethiopia's Emperor Is Deposed

On September 11, 1974, soldiers and police arrested members of the imperial family in various parts of Ethiopia. By the next morning, military units had strengthened their hold on the capital, Addis Ababa. Tanks and jeeps surrounded the emperor's Jubilee Palace. A group of officers, armed with submachine guns, entered the building and confronted their 82-year-old sovereign, Haile Selassie. The leader of the group, Major Debela Dinsa, accused the emperor of abusing his power and declared that his reign was over. Then Haile Selassie was escorted to a car – not one of his own limousines but, humiliatingly, a small Volkswagen Beetle. The fallen emperor was driven away and held at a military barracks.

The emperor's career

This ended Haile Selassie's remarkable career. As emperor of Ethiopia from 1930, he had tried to modernize his large, ancient, but poor country. Then, in 1935, Italy's fascist dictator Benito Mussolini decided to conquer Ethiopia and turn it into a colony. The Ethiopians conducted a brave but hopeless struggle against the invaders, and in 1936, Haile Selassie was forced into exile. He was restored to the throne in 1941, during World War

Haile Selassie and his bodyguards during the most heroic period of the emperor's career, the 1935 invasion of Ethiopia by Italy.

What the papers said

The dismal latter part of Haile Selassie's internal policies should not obscure his earlier career. He led resistance to the Italian invasion of 1935. He unified the country, and initiated early reforms. But he stayed too long. The ex-Emperor['s] ... attitude ... made it impossible for him to understand why education and handouts of land, food, and money were regarded not just as gifts ... but as rights. He never understood why these whetted rather than satisfied appetites ... he became increasingly out of touch ... and for service to his people substituted corruption and ... expensive political patronage.

Guardian, September 13, 1974

The Ethiopian emperor Haile Selassie in old age, a few months before he was overthrown. Under his rule, Ethiopia remained a desperately poor country. However, those who took power after him were no more successful.

II. His dignified resistance to the Italians made him a hero to many Africans. When the colonial era ended, he became one of the founders of the Organization of African Unity, with its headquarters at Addis Ababa.

Failure and fall

However, Haile Selassie failed to solve Ethiopia's problems. The country remained poor even by African standards. A minority of land-owning families held all real power, and little progress was made toward democracy. In 1960, Ethiopia took over neighboring Eritrea, and fierce Eritrean resistance locked the Ethiopian army into a long and costly struggle. When drought and famine struck central Ethiopia, the emperor's government mishandled the situation. Corrupt officials stole resources intended for starving people, and many thousands died.

By February 1974, the country was suffering from inflation and unemployment. The armed forces began to take over. Haile Selassie became increasingly isolated and powerless, and few were surprised when he was deposed. In August 1975, his death was announced; he may have been murdered by his captors. Ethiopia was ruled by a military committee, the Dergue, and then by the ruthless Major Mengistu Haile Mariam. Years of tyranny, fruitless wars, and chaos followed until Mengistu's regime collapsed in 1991.

- **SEE ALSO**
  Pages 26–27: November 20, 1975
  General Franco Dies

- **FURTHER INFORMATION**
  Books:
  Ethiopia by Andrew Campbell (Watts, 2006)
  Websites:
  www.time.com/time/magazine/article/
  0,9171,908740,00.html
  "The End of the Lion of Judah"

29 APRIL 1975

Saigon Falls to the North Vietnamese

By April 29, 1975, the war was as good as over. The South Vietnamese army had collapsed and the forces of communist North Vietnam were poised to take Saigon, the capital of the South. Many people had fled from the city, and abandoned foreign embassies were being looted. However, the U.S. embassy was still occupied. It was a fortress protected by high walls, barbed wire, and a contingent of U.S. Marines.

Dramatic events were unfolding there. The embassy compound was crowded with Americans and Vietnamese, desperate to leave the country. Many more Vietnamese were outside, frantically trying to climb in. One after another, U.S. helicopters landed in the compound and, dangerously overcrowded, carried their passengers to aircraft carriers waiting off the coast. Hours later, North Vietnamese tanks reached the center of Saigon and the South's president surrendered unconditionally.

As the Vietnam War comes to an end, South Vietnamese line up, waving identity documents, to board a bus that will take them to the U.S. Embassy and, they hope, safety.

The long struggle

The communist victory ended a conflict that went back to a time when Vietnam was a French colony. By the 1950s, the country was divided into independent northern and southern states. A new struggle began in which South Vietnam came under attack from communist guerrillas inside the country, unofficially backed by North Vietnam. The United States intervened to support South Vietnam and found itself pouring in more and more troops and arms. As the 1960s went on, U.S. casualties mounted. Despite its huge firepower and devastating bombing raids on the North, the United States seemed unable to win. Many Americans began to oppose the war, and the country became bitterly divided. Finally, the United States and North

Vietnam made peace, and by 1973 the United States had withdrawn all its forces. The war between North and South went on, however, and it became clear that U.S. efforts to strengthen the South Vietnamese army had failed. The victorious North Vietnamese surged forward to take Saigon.

Pol Pot's atrocities

In the same year, 1975, communist forces took control of two neighboring ex-French colonies, Cambodia and Laos. For them, and for Vietnam, rebuilding a devastated country was an immense task. But in Cambodia worse was to come. Led by Pol Pot, the communist Khmer Rouge introduced brutal and radical policies that uprooted huge numbers of people. At least a million Cambodians were killed by the regime or starved in the chaotic conditions it created.

Their ordeal only ended in 1979 when the Vietnamese invaded the country and set up a less extreme government.

A pile of skulls, part of the Choeng Ek Memorial in Cambodia. It was set up to remember the countless victims of the Khmer Rouge regime, which ruled the country 1975–79.

⊙ eye witness

As the first Chinook helicopter made its precarious landing, its rotors slashed into a tree, and the snapping branches sounded like gunfire.... The helicopter's capacity was fifty [people], but it lifted off with seventy. The pilot's skill was breathtaking.... At six-fifteen p.m. it was my turn.... The helicopter tilted, rose, dropped sharply, then climbed as if laden with rocks.... There was small-arms fire around us, but they were letting us go; and when the South China Sea lay beneath us, the pilot, who was red-eyed with fatigue ... lit up a cigarette and handed the packet around.

John Pilger, The Last Day (Mirror Group Books, 1975)

• **SEE ALSO**
Pages 6–7: December 16, 1971
Bangladesh is Born
Pages 36–37: February 1, 1979
Ayatollah Khomeini Returns to Iran

• **FURTHER INFORMATION**
📖 Books:
The Fall of Saigon by Michael V Uschan (Heinemann, 2002)
🖱 Websites:
http://www.usskawishiwi.org/Vietnam/Saigon-1975.html
Exciting photographs of the U.S. embassy evacuation

General Franco Dies

Following several heart attacks and severe peritonitis, Spain's 83-year-old dictator, Francisco Franco, died on November 20, 1975. As Franco had intended, Prince Juan Carlos became king of Spain and the new head of state. Franco had supervised Juan Carlos's education and hoped that the king would uphold the political system. However, Franco's followers suspected – rightly – that Juan Carlos wanted a democratic monarchy. Many of them held powerful positions, so the political situation was tense and complicated.

The dictatorship

Franco had established his dictatorship in 1939 at the end of a ferocious civil war. His regime combined traditional conservative and Catholic values with elements of Fascism inspired by Franco's onetime allies, Fascist Italy and Nazi Germany. During his 36-year rule, the liberals, socialists, and communists who had opposed him in the Civil War were mercilessly hounded. In the 1970s, Spain was still a country in which political parties, independent trade unions, strikes, and free elections were forbidden.

The coffined body of Francisco Franco, the general who won the Spanish Civil War and was dictator of Spain from 1939 until his death in 1975.

Stealthy change

By this time, Franco's Spain was out of step with the rest of prosperous, democratic Western Europe. In 1974, a revolution in neighboring Portugal overthrew the only other dictatorship in the region. But even after Franco's death, it was hard to bring about change in Spain because of the carefully constructed system he had left behind him. Juan Carlos moved cautiously, working within the existing laws. A direct move toward democracy, however popular, risked a coup by military leaders loyal to their old chief. Without denouncing Franco, Juan Carlos maneuvered for months to replace followers of the dictator who held key positions. The decisive moment came in July 1976, when the king was able to name a liberal-minded official, Adolfo Suárez, as his prime minister. Political parties were legalized and free elections were held. By the end of 1978, the Francoist state was being dismantled and a new, democratic constitution had been drawn up and approved.

The failed coup

The early years of democratic Spain were troubled, and in February 1981 the long-feared coup attempt occurred. Civil Guards (military-style police) seized the parliament building and held its members as hostages. But the king and millions of demonstrators condemned the coup, which rapidly collapsed. The episode showed that democracy had taken a firm hold in Spain. This was confirmed in 1982 when the Socialist Party won the elections and was able to take office peacefully.

King Juan Carlos I of Spain signs the country's 1978 constitution. It ended the political system set up by Franco and made Spain a fully democratic state.

What the papers said

While the official condolences were going on, first reports said that the announcement of the dictator's death brought an explosion of joy…. In one street in a fashionable part of Madrid while mass for Franco was being held in the church, less than 100 yards away a popular bar was packed with smiling and laughing people drinking to the dawn of a new era free from fascism…. Abroad, despite the spate of official condolences, there was hardly a personal tribute among them, and there was a chorus of hope for future democracy in Spain.

Sam Russell, *Morning Star*, November 21, 1975

• **SEE ALSO**
  Pages 22–23: September 12, 1974
  Ethiopia's Emperor Is Deposed

• **FURTHER INFORMATION**
  📖 Books:
  Spain by Nathaniel Harris (Raintree, 2004)
  Websites:
  http://countrystudies.us/spain/25.htm
  The post-Franco era and Spanish history
  in general

Concorde Goes into Service

Aircraft capable of supersonic flight – faster than the speed of sound – had been manufactured since 1947. But such aircraft had always been built for military purposes. Concorde was something new and thrilling – an airliner that could hold one hundred passengers and travel across oceans and continents while cruising at 1,335 miles (2,150 kilometres) an hour, twice the speed of sound. Concorde was a joint venture, developed and funded by the British and French governments. So the first passenger flights were arranged to begin simultaneously in the two countries.

British Airways' Concorde 206 lifts off from Heathrow Airport on its first passenger flight to Bahrain. At the same time an Air France Concorde took off from Paris for Rio de Janeiro.

On January 21, 1976, British Airways' Concorde 206 left Heathrow Airport for Bahrain in the Persian Gulf. Air France flew from Orly Airport, via Dakar in Senegal, to Rio de Janeiro in Brazil. Flights to the United States were not immediately possible because of objections to the sonic boom, the explosive sound heard when the aircraft broke the sound barrier. The objections were overcome, and from November 1977 the daily flights from Paris and London to New York became the most important

The end of the Concorde story, November 2003. With Concorde about to retire, one of the British Airways' fleet is towed toward lower Manhattan, where it will be given an honored place in New York's Intrepid Sea, Air & Space Museum.

part of Concorde's schedule. The transatlantic crossing usually took about three and a half hours, at least twice as fast as conventional, "subsonic" aircraft. Because the world is divided into different time zones, when Concordes traveled westward, they arrived at a clock time earlier than the one at which they had left!

The striking, birdlike image of Concorde's distinctive "droop" nose and double-delta-shaped wings became known all over the world. These were functional as well as attractive features, typical of the aircraft's advanced technology. Worked on all through the 1960s and test-flown from 1969, Concorde was an expensive project. The original intention was to sell the aircraft to the airlines of other countries, but events such as the 1973 oil crisis put off potential customers. In the long run, Britain and France probably benefited from their exclusive right to Concorde's prestige. During their lifetime, Concordes set a number of world speed records. There was a single serious accident in 2000, when a crash at Gonesse in France killed 113 people. This was a factor in the decision to retire Concorde. Its farewell flight, on November 26, 2003, marked the end of an impressive and glamorous career.

⊙ **eye** witness

On January 21, 1976 I stood with my wife, camera at the ready, at the take-off end of runway 28L.... Around us were crowds of people, some wearing ... "service" earphones connected to electronic devices wired up to microphones on poles. Concorde would not start ... unrecorded! We listened to a local radio broadcast. At 11:40 precisely the commentator announced that Concorde had begun to roll. Next came the distinctive sound of the four reheated Olympus engines. Then Concorde GBOAA came in view, climbing out over the approach lights of the reciprocal runway, with the undercarriage retracting. Commercial supersonic services had begun.

**Christopher Orlebar, *The Concorde Story*
(Osprey, 2004)**

- **SEE ALSO**
  Pages 30–31: July 20, 1976
  Viking 1 Lands on Mars

- **FURTHER INFORMATION**
  📖 Books:
  Concorde by Suzanne J. Murdico
  (Children's Press, 2001)
  ☞ Websites:
  www.britishairways.com/concorde/index.html
  British Airways' Celebrating Concorde website

Viking 1 Lands on Mars

Viking 1 and Viking 2 were American space probes – unmanned craft despatched by NASA, the organization that ran the U.S. space program. Each probe consisted of an orbiter, designed to keep flying steadily round the planet, and a lander that would descend to the surface. Both orbiters and landers were able to send images and data back to earth. If the landers remained operational after reaching the surface of Mars, they would provide the first close-up views of a planet that had always had a romantic and mysterious reputation.

The first images

On July 20, Viking 1's lander arrived intact on the surface. Within days, the images it sent back to earth had been processed and published. It also sent back analyses of soil samples and other data. The lander had set down on an irregular, cratered area, and so Viking 2's descent was rescheduled so that it could land on more suitable terrain. It came down on the other side of the planet in September 1976. The Viking images showed a dry, dusty, rock-strewn surface, and the data they sent back gave no support to the often expressed idea that Mars was, or had once been, capable of sustaining life. However, there were other possibilities to explore, and speculation has continued to the present day.

An image of the dry, rocky surface of the planet Mars, sent back to earth by the U.S. probe Viking Lander 2. Part of the lander can be seen at the front of the picture.

Further into space

In 1969, the United States scored an immense triumph by putting its astronauts on the moon. Other moon flights followed until 1972, but further exploration of the solar system could only be carried out by unmanned craft. The rival superpowers, the United States and the Soviet Union, continued to dominate space exploration. In 1974, NASA's Mariner 10 flew past Mercury, the planet nearest the sun. The following year, the Soviet probe Venera 9 landed on the surface of Venus, long hidden from astronomers beneath dense clouds, and sent back the first images. The United States then sent probes on much longer journeys, toward the outer planets of the solar system.

Space stations and satellites

Meanwhile, astronauts found a new role in the space stations that had begun orbiting the earth. Salyut 1, launched in 1971, was the first of a series of Soviet stations, followed in 1973 by the U.S. station Skylab. Space stations were used primarily for scientific research, but by the end of the 1970s many other artificial satellites were orbiting the earth, used for many purposes, including telephone and TV communications and military spying.

A dramatic view of the Skylab space station, taken from space by the associated Skylab 4 mission. Skylab was the first U.S. space station, visited by human crews and orbiting the earth from 1973 to 1979.

⊙ eye witness

Mike Carr recalled his feelings when the ... team members began to look at the ... data in detail. "We were just astounded – both a mixture of elation and shock." They were elated at the quality and detail of the pictures but shocked at what they saw. All their data-processing schedules had been based on a preconceived notion of what Mars should look like, and this was not it.... All that they saw – the etched surfaces, the multitude of craters and islands in the channels ... told them that the ... site was not a suitable place to land.

E. C. and L. N. Ezell, *On Mars: Exploration of the Red Planet 1958–1978* (NASA History Series, 1984)

- **SEE ALSO**
  Pages 28–29: January 21, 1976
  Concorde Goes into Service

- **FURTHER INFORMATION**
  📖 Books:
  Mars by Giles Sparrow (Heinemann, 2001)
  🖱 Websites:
  news.bbc.co.uk/onthisday/hi/dates/stories/july/20/newsid_2515000/2515447.stm
  BBC "On This Day" feature, linked with "Exploring Mars"

14

JULY

1977

The Sex Pistols on Top of the Pops

On July 14, 1977, a video of the Sex Pistols was shown on Britain's leading pop TV program, *Top of the Pops*. The group had now definitely become mainstream national performers. Their rise to fame had begun only two years earlier when they played their first gig as the Sex Pistols with Johnny Rotten as lead singer. Their harsh, driving punk rock style matched the angrily rebellious mood of songs like "Anarchy in the UK" and "God Save the Queen," which described Queen Elizabeth II as reigning over a "fascist regime." In December 1976, the group had become notorious through a TV program in which one of them, encouraged by the interviewer, had sworn profusely. Many people were outraged by the Sex Pistols and they were banned at some venues. But they made headlines. Despite protests, *Top of the Pops* showed them performing their latest hit, "Pretty Vacant," dedicated to British youth.

International punk

Punk was a lifestyle as well as a type of music. Its young fans – punks – had their own distinctive look, with short, spiky hair and torn, safety-pin-decorated clothes. Both the music and the style first took shape in New York. Rock music had always had a wild, rebellious image, but by the early 1970s "glam rock" and "prog rock" had developed in a more showy, elaborate, technique-conscious direction.

However, some bands had continued to play in harder, more direct styles, inspiring punk performers such as Patti Smith and the Ramones who began to make their mark in 1974. Punk spread across the United States and became an international trend, not only in Britain

What the papers said

Various singers caressed the hand-mike with drooling narcissism [self-love], as though it were a stick of lip salve. The comically horrendous Sex Pistols on Thursday's *Top of the Pops* (BBC1) turned the same device into a Black and Decker power drill. They "sang" like a group that wanted to punch holes in your knee-caps. The day cannot be too long delayed when showbiz will start doling out Death Achievement Awards, a prize to be won after making as many people as possible as sick as possible in no less time than it takes to pierce an ear-lobe with a safety-pin.

Dennis Potter, *The Sunday Times*, July 17, 1977

*The British band
the Sex Pistols,
fronted by Johnny
Rotten, performs
in the United States.
The band made a
highly controversial
impact.*

(the Sex Pistols, the Clash,
the Damned) but in Australia (the Saints),
Canada (the Diodes), and Western Europe.

After punk

Having changed the direction of popular music, punk continued to
evolve. In January 1978, the Sex Pistols broke up, while new or
re-formed bands were appearing all the time. One trend was
represented by hardcore in the United States and Oi! and anarcho-
punk in Britain. It went even further in presenting aggressive
political messages, and the discordant sound and shouted lyrics
deliberately rejected traditional musical skills and melody.
By contrast, New Wave and Pop Punk moved closer to
popular and dance music, allowing bands such as
Blondie and Talking Heads to achieve mainstream
success. Revived from time to time, punk influenced
later anti-mainstream trends such as alternative rock
and indie (music on independent labels).

FURTHER INFORMATION

Books:
1970s Pop by Bob Brunning (Heinemann, 1998)

Websites:
www.rockhall.com/inductee/sex-pistols
An interesting Rock and Roll Hall of Fame site

Karol Wojtyla Is Elected Pope

The pope is the head of the worldwide Roman Catholic Church. He rules Vatican City, a tiny independent state in Rome, the capital of Italy. When a pope dies, the College of Cardinals (leading churchmen) meets in the Sistine Chapel in the Vatican to elect his successor. There are usually several ballots (voting sessions) before one of the candidates receives enough support to be declared the new pope.

A surprise choice

The election is a dramatic event. Black smoke rises from the chapel chimney after each unsuccessful ballot; when the smoke is white, the world knows that the choice has been made. A huge crowd waits eagerly for the result in Rome's St. Peter's Square. The election in October 1978 was decided after eight ballots held over two days. White smoke rose from the chapel window at 6:18 P.M. on October 16. The cardinals' choice was a surprise – 58-year-old Karol Wojtyla, archbishop of Krakow in Poland. He was the first-ever Polish pope and the first non-Italian in 455 years. When elected, a pope chooses the name he wishes to be known by. Wojtyla wished to pay tribute to his frail predecessor, John Paul I, whose reign lasted only 33 days. The new pope became John Paul II.

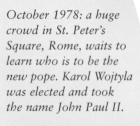

October 1978: a huge crowd in St. Peter's Square, Rome, waits to learn who is to be the new pope. Karol Wojtyla was elected and took the name John Paul II.

Papal globe-trotter

One of his first actions broke with tradition. Instead of a few words in Latin, John Paul II, master of many languages, spoke eloquently in Italian to the delighted crowd in St. Peter's Square. This popular touch proved to be typical. Previous popes had traveled very little, but John Paul II visited over one hundred countries all over the world. He was greeted by vast crowds and moved among them, standing up in a specially designed car, the "popemobile." He made an extraordinary personal impact on both Catholics and non-Catholics. This public exposure was not risk-free. There were several attempts to assassinate him, notably in 1981 when he was seriously wounded by a gunman.

John Paul II preached international peace and reconciliation between religions. Yet his reign had controversial aspects. For example, he strongly asserted traditional teachings on topics such as contraception, felt by some sections of the Church to need modernizing. John Paul II lived to see the end of communism in his native Poland and the rest of Eastern Europe. His long reign ended with his death in 2005.

A smiling Pope John Paul II is greeted by adoring crowds during his weekly general audience in St. Peter's Church, Rome.

eye witness

I defended my opinion openly before the conclave. I said that "It's time to change the system and to vote for a non-Italian".... There was enormous tension the whole time.... When the number of votes for him [Wojtyla] approached one-half [of the votes needed to elect him] he cast away his pencil and sat up straight. He was red in the face. Then he was holding his head in his hands. My impression was that he was completely confused. Then the final majority number turned up. He had two-thirds of the vote plus one.

Cardinal Franz König, quoted in Tad Szulc, *Pope John Paul II* (Scribner, 1995)

• **FURTHER INFORMATION**
📖 Books:
Pope John Paul II by Peggy Burns (Wayland, 2001)
🔗 Websites:
www.catholic-pages.com/pope/election.asp
A full description of how popes are elected

Ayatollah Khomeini Returns to Iran

After 15 years of exile, the 78-year-old Ayatollah Khomeini flew into Tehran, the capital of Iran. As his title, ayatollah, indicated, he was a senior Muslim religious figure. But for Iranians he was above all a symbol of popular resistance to the shah (king) of Iran, who had been overthrown two weeks earlier. The situation was still chaotic, and the stern, bearded Khomeini was hailed as a savior. On his arrival, a million people greeted him rapturously, brandishing his picture.

Returned from exile, Ayatollah Khomeini is acclaimed at his home by his massed supporters.

Iran under the shah

Iran was one of several Middle Eastern countries in which modern and traditional lifestyles coexisted uneasily. It was an oil-rich country, making substantial, if uneven, economic progress. Until 1979, the shah seemed an impressive figure, internationally admired for modernizing his country. But in Iran his modernizing, and his close ties to the United States, outraged traditionalists like the Ayatollah Khomeini, who was exiled for opposing greater freedom for women and other reforms. At the same time, liberals and other pro-reform groups were angered by the lack of democracy in Iran. The shah held absolute power, and his secret police, SAVAK, were notorious for torturing and murdering the regime's opponents.

The revolution

The shah appeared to be in complete control until January 1979, when an official newspaper published an attack on the exiled Khomeini. Some demonstrators protested, troops fired on them, and street demonstrations spread all over the country. The shah mishandled the situation. He used enough force to anger people but not enough to repress them, and the concessions he made came too late. The situation spiraled out of control, and the shah fled the country on January 16, 1979.

The Islamic Republic

Soon after Khomeini's return, Iran was proclaimed an Islamic Republic. The Muslim religion had become a major political force. Then the shah, who had cancer, was admitted to the United States. Most Iranians believed that the United States was plotting with the shah, and in November 1979, Iranian students took over the U.S. embassy in Tehran and held its staff as hostages. Anti-American feeling swept Iran, the moderate government resigned, and liberal and other secular groups were swept aside. Iran became a state in which ayatollahs supervised the government, and society was dominated by conservative Islamic ideas and practices (Islamic fundamentalism). The 1980s saw Iran become a revolutionary force in the Muslim world, hostile to the United States and the West.

Iranians stand on top of the U.S. embassy wall and burn an American flag. Seizing the embassy and taking hostages from its staff, students set off a crisis that lasted until 1981.

eye witness

Despite the prospect of serious days ahead, yesterday was one of celebration and jubilation for the followers of the man whom some see as a mystical Imam, or leader.... Throughout the city, people climbed trees or perched on the tops of bus shelters, telephone boxes, garden walls or railings to get a glimpse of Khomeini. His portrait was everywhere, on walls and windows, strung across streets and on pennants waved by the crowds. It was a welcome reminiscent of ... Hollywood films depicting the return of a Roman Emperor ... but instead of a cast of thousands it had a cast of millions.

James Allen, *Daily Telegraph*, February 2, 1979

- **SEE ALSO**
  Pages 6–7: December 16, 1971
  Bangladesh is Born
  Pages 24–25: April 29, 1975
  Saigon Falls to the North Vietnamese

- **FURTHER INFORMATION**
  Books:
  Iran and the Islamic Revolution by John King (Heinemann, 2005)
  Websites:
  www.time.com/time/time100/leaders/profile/khomeini3.html
  A good summary of Khomeini's life and career

Soviet Forces Enter Afghanistan

It began when thousands of airborne Soviet troops were landed at the airport outside Kabul, the capital of Afghanistan. The communist Afghan government was facing a major rebellion and had been asking its Soviet allies to send troops and military supplies since early 1979. But the Soviets had plans of their own. On December 27, Soviet units occupied key points in Kabul and stormed the presidential palace. The president, Hafizullah Amin, was killed and another communist, Babrak Karmal, was installed as the new leader. Karmal, too, needed Soviet help, and ground troops poured into the country from the north.

Afghan President Hafizullah Amin holds a press conference. Having seized power, he was soon to be overthrown himself.

Communist Afghanistan

Afghanistan was a poor, economically backward Muslim country in which local and tribal loyalties were strong. Communism seemed unlikely to win wide support in such a society, despite the influence of Afghanistan's mighty neighbor, the Soviet Union. However, in April 1978, the Afghan army overthrew the existing regime and the communist PDPA (People's Democratic Party of Afghanistan) took over the government. Its policies sparked a series of rebellions that were soon being funded and supplied by the United States. At first the Soviet leaders were reluctant to intervene and sent only limited military assistance. However, they came to believe that Amin's brutal methods were making the situation worse and that the United States might move in, possibly after doing

⊙ eye witness

I returned again [to Afghanistan] as a journalist in the autumn of 1979…. Outwardly, the Afghan capital appeared quite normal…. Nevertheless, the tension, the insecurity, the growing hatred for the communists were apparent just beneath the surface…. With the growth of repression ... and the fighting constantly spreading to new fronts in the countryside, it was evident that something would have to break sooner or later; another coup perhaps, an army uprising, or even a rebel takeover of Kabul. Few people expected anything as drastic as the Soviet intervention.

Edward R. Girardit, *Afghanistan: The Soviet War*
(Croom Helm, 1985)

A group of Afghan fighters, part of the resistance to the communist regime and the Soviet army. With U.S. help they rapidly became much better armed.

a deal with Amin himself. Consequently, the Soviets replaced Amin with Karmal, the leader of a rival faction in the PDPA. Within a few months, there were 80,000 Soviet troops in Afghanistan, and the rebel groups that tried to resist them in open warfare were crushed with ruthless efficiency.

A Soviet blunder

Nevertheless, the Soviet intervention in Afghanistan was a serious mistake. The United States and its allies denounced it as an invasion, and most of the Muslim world was angered. During the 1970s, relations between the superpowers had improved, but the Afghanistan issue led to renewed hostility, which persisted into the 1980s. The Soviets' early military successes failed to end Afghan resistance, and groups of guerrillas, known as mujahideen (warriors), began to use hit-and-run tactics against Soviet and government forces. This proved highly effective in Afghanistan's mountainous terrain. For the Soviets, Afghanistan soon turned into a nightmare, often compared with the demoralizing U.S. involvement in Vietnam. Afghanistan itself would become a flashpoint in world politics for decades to come.

- **SEE ALSO**
  Pages 12–13: September 11, 1973
  Chile's Government Is Overthrown
  Pages 24–25: April 29, 1975
  Saigon Falls to the North Vietnamese

- **FURTHER INFORMATION**
  📖 Books:
  The Afghan Rebels by D. J. Herda (Watts, 1990)
  🖱 Websites:
  www.globalresearch.ca/articles/BRZ110A.html
  A revealing interview with a U.S. presidential adviser

May
4
1970

Protesting Students Are Killed at Kent State

Antiwar protests were common on college campuses in the 1960s and early 1970s, as students demonstrated against U.S. involvement in Vietnam. On May 4, 1970, a protest at Kent State University in Kent, Ohio, turned tragic when members of the Ohio National Guard shot and killed four students. The event further split a nation that was already divided by political and social events.

Lead-up to tragedy

When Richard Nixon was elected president in 1968, he vowed to end the war in Vietnam. On April 30, 1970, however, Nixon announced that the United States and South Vietnam were invading Cambodia and that more Americans would be drafted. Many Americans were outraged by this escalation of the war. Demonstrations were held on many campuses on May 1, including Kent State. After people threw bottles at cars and broke store windows in downtown Kent, the mayor declared a state of emergency and asked the governor to send in the National Guard to help maintain order. At a demonstration on May 2, a campus building was set on fire.

On May 4, 2,000 people gathered for a noon rally. National Guard troops, armed with rifles and bayonets, used tear gas in an attempt to disperse the students, who responded by chanting, cursing, and throwing rocks. Without warning, 28 Guardsmen fired up to 67 shots at the students, killing four. Two were taking part in the protest, but the other two were just walking by. Nine other students were wounded, including one who was permanently paralyzed. The Guard later claimed that a sniper had shot at them, but no evidence was found.

National Guard troops march across Kent State campus in an effort to contain the protest. Shortly afterward, they opened fire on the demonstrators.

Reaction and aftermath

News of the shootings quickly spread. In the next days, almost 500 U.S. colleges and universities were shut down or disrupted by student protests. On June 13, Nixon announced the formation of the President's Commission on Campus Unrest. The commission concluded that at Kent State, "the indiscriminate firing of rifles into a crowd of students and the deaths that followed were unnecessary, unwarranted, and inexcusable."

Memorials were established at Kent State, dedicated to the students who died, and a ceremony is held each year on May 4. A center to study peaceful methods of dealing with conflict was also set up, but the wounds that had been inflicted upon the nation, and those at Kent State, did not heal quickly.

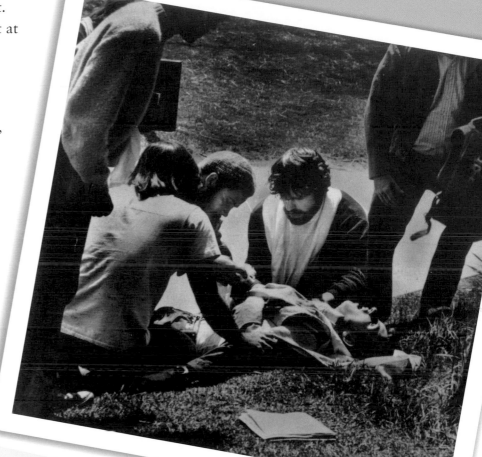

Kent State students gather aound a wounded student who was shot by National Guard troops during the May 4 protests.

What the papers said

The crackle of the rifle volley cut the suddenly still air. It appeared to go on, as a solid volley, for perhaps a full minute or a little longer. Some of the students dived to the ground, crawling on the grass in terror. Others stood shocked or half crouched . . . . Near the top of the hill . . . , a student crumpled over, spun sideways and fell to the ground, shot in the head. When the firing stopped, a slim girl, wearing a cowboy shirt and faded jeans, was lying face down on the road at the edge of the parking lot, blood pouring out . . . , about 10 feet from this reporter.

John Kifner, New York Times, May 5, 1970

• FURTHER INFORMATION

📖 Books:
The Kent State Shootings by Natalie M. Rosinsky (Compass Point Books, 2008)

🖰 Websites:
www.may4.org
The Kent State May 4 Center

Abortion Is Declared Legal

On January 22, 1973, the U.S. Supreme Court issued one of its most important and controversial decisions, in the case of *Roe v. Wade*. The Court ruled that women have a constitutional right to have an abortion.

Changing Laws and Beliefs

During the early history of the United States, abortions (terminations of pregnancy) were legal and done on a regular basis. In the late 1800s, however, different states began to pass laws making the procedure a crime. By the late 1950s, there were increasing efforts to make abortion legal. Many people believed that women should have control over their bodies and have reproductive rights. People were also roused by horror stories about women who had undergone illegal abortions. Wealthy women could pay for safe abortions, but many women had to resort to dangerous methods. Many women died or had serious complications. In 1970, four states – Alaska, Hawaii, New York, and Washington – repealed their laws and allowed abortion on demand.

Norma McCorvey, who was known as "Jane Roe" during the landmark Roe v. Wade lawsuit of 1973. She revealed her true identity in the 1980s.

A Landmark Case

In 1970, a Texas woman named Norma McCorvey wanted to have an abortion, which was against Texas law. Her lawyers called her "Jane Roe" to protect her privacy, and they sued Henry Wade, the Dallas County district attorney, to challenge the law. A federal district court in Texas ruled that the law was unconstitutional. That decision was then appealed to the U.S. Supreme Court.

On January 22, 1973, the Court ruled, 7–2, that state laws that prohibit abortion were unconstitutional. The Court set down guidelines under which abortions could be performed. In the first trimester (three months) of pregnancy, a woman could have an abortion on demand. During the second trimester, states could regulate abortion but not prohibit it. During the third trimester, states could forbid abortions unless the woman's life was in danger. The Court based its decision on the belief that laws against abortion violated a woman's constitutional right to privacy.

The decision did not end the debate on abortion. Both "pro-choice" and "pro-life" organizations crusade for their side. Candidates for political office are questioned about their stand on abortion. In addition, many states have passed laws that permitted abortions but made them difficult to obtain. A number of cases on the newer abortion laws have reached the Supreme Court. While the Court has not overturned its decision in Roe, it has upheld various abortion restrictions.

On January 22, 2008 – the 35th anniversary of Roe v. Wade – anti-abortion activists make their annual "March for Life" protest in Washington, D.C.

 eye witness

I am a retired gynecologist. . . . My early formal training . . . was spent in New York City, from 1948 to 1953 . . . . There I saw and treated almost every complication of illegal abortion that one could conjure . . . . It is important to remember that *Roe v. Wade* did not mean that abortions could be performed. They have always been done, dating from ancient Greek days. What *Roe* said was that ending a pregnancy could be carried out by medical personnel, in a medically accepted setting, thus conferring on women, finally, the full rights of first-class citizens – and freeing their doctors to treat them as such.

Waldo L. Fielding, M.D., *New York Times*, June 3, 2008

● **FURTHER INFORMATION**

📖 **Books:**

Roe v. Wade: Protecting a Woman's Right to Choose by Susan Tyler Hitchcock (Chelsea House, 2006)

Websites:

www.landmarkcases.org/roe/home.html
Landmark Supreme Court Cases: Roe v. Wade
www.npr.org/news/specials/roevwade/index.html
30th Anniversary of Roe v. Wade—Series by National Public Radio

Nuclear Accident Occurs at Three Mile Island

In the predawn hours of March 28, 1979, a pump stopped working at the Three Mile Island nuclear power plant, located near Middletown, Pennsylvania. It was a simple malfunction, but it was followed by a series of other equipment failures and worker errors, resulting in the worst accident in the history of the U.S. nuclear power industry.

An aerial view of the Three Mile Island nuclear power plant, showing its four cooling towers.

A Series of Events

The Three Mile Island nuclear power plant had two pressurized water reactors, generating electricity. At the time of the accident, Unit 1 was shut down for refueling. Unit 2, where the accident occurred, had been in operation only three months. At 4 A.M. on March 28, a pump in the plant's main cooling system failed. This led to a series of events that caused the core of the reactor to overheat. Workers could not figure out what had gone wrong, and they took steps that actually made things worse. Eventually, investigators determined that half of the core melted during the early stages of the accident.

Shortly after the incident began, plant managers notified officials in the community, at the Nuclear Regulatory Commission (NRC), and at the White House that there was a problem at Three Mile Island. NRC inspectors rushed to the scene, and efforts were made to control the situation. When radioactive gas and steam continued to build up, workers were forced to vent the gas into the atmosphere. In addition, they discovered that a potentially hazardous hydrogen bubble was building in the reactor core.

On March 30, Pennsylvania Governor Richard Thornburgh urged everyone living within 10 miles (17 kilometers) of the plant to stay indoors. Later that day, he advised pregnant women and young children to leave the area. This caused widespread fear, and more than 140,000 people decided to evacuate. The crisis ended on April 1, when it became clear that the hydrogen bubble would not burn or explode. People began returning to the area later that week.

Long-Term Consequences

Experts stated that the radiation that entered the atmosphere was very low. Studies showed no negative effects on people, plants, or animals. Nevertheless, public mistrust of the nuclear industry grew. The NRC increased its regulatory oversight, and changes were made in such areas as emergency response planning, training, and the creation of safeguards. At Three Mile Island today, the Unit 1 reactor continues to operate, but Unit 2 is permanently shut down.

Left to right: the NCR's Harold Denton, Governor Thornburgh, President and Mrs Carter, and a plant official at Three Mile Island on April 1, 1979.

What the report said

Many public officials learned of the accident from the news media .... Harrisburg [Pennsylvania] Mayor Paul Doutrich .... heard about the problem in a 9:15 A.M. telephone call from a radio station in Boston. "They asked me what we were doing about the nuclear emergency," Doutrich recalled. "My response was, 'What nuclear emergency?' They said, 'Well, at Three Mile Island.' 'I know nothing about it. We have a nuclear plant there, but I know nothing about a problem.' So they told me; a Boston radio station."

From the Report of the President's Commission on the Accident at Three Mile Island, October 30, 1979

• **FURTHER INFORMATION**

📖 **Books:**
Meltdown: A Race Against Nuclear Disaster at Three Mile Island—A Reporter's Story by Wilborn Hampton (Candlewick Press, 2001)

🖱 **Websites:**
www.pbs.org/wgbh.amex/three
American Experience: Meltdown at Three Mile Island, companion site for a TV film presented on the Public Broadcasting System

People of the Decade

Muhammad Ali
(born 1942)
American boxer Muhammad Ali was the only heavyweight to win the world championship three times. Originally known as Cassius Clay, he took the name Muhammad Ali when he converted to the Nation of Islam (Black Muslims). He was world champion 1964–1971, 1974–1978, and 1978–1979. For a heavyweight, Ali was unusually skillful and fast on his feet, as well as strong. An entertaining personality, he boasted amusingly in rhyme, but his most celebrated statement was "I am the greatest!"

Idi Amin
(1924–2003)
A former British army officer, Idi Amin became chief of the Ugandan armed forces (1966–1970). In January 1971, he overthrew the government and made himself president. Apparently clownish, Amin proved to be a blood-thirsty tyrant. Ugandans of Asian descent were thrown out of the country, and many thousands of people from tribes that Amin disliked were tortured and killed. In 1979, following a successful invasion by Tanzanian forces and Ugandan rebels, Amin fled the country, dying in exile.

David Bowie
(born 1947)
The British rock singer, song writer and actor was at the height of his celebrity in the 1970s. His breakthrough second album was *Hunky Dory* (1971). Bowie mixed and varied musical styles, from glam rock to heavy metal. Bizarre titles (*The Rise and Fall of Ziggy Stardust and the Spiders from Mars*) were matched by Bowie's deliberately extreme self-presentation, for example heavily made up. Bowie's best-known film performance was as an alien in *The Man Who Fell to Earth* (1976).

Leonid Illych Brezhnev
(1906–1982)
Brezhnev was the leader of the Soviet Union from 1964, when he ousted Nikita Khrushchev. All through the 1970s the Soviet Union seemed formidable, but Brezhnev's attempts to match the United States in armaments and international influence were in fact seriously weakening it. Brezhnev and other aging Soviet leaders failed to reform the stagnating economy, and the 1979 Soviet intervention in Afghanistan proved to be another serious mistake, contributing toward the eventual collapse of the Soviet Union in 1991.

Jimmy Carter
(born 1920)
U.S. politician Jimmy Carter, a Democrat, became president in 1977. Carter played a leading role in making peace between Egypt and Israel. He strongly opposed Soviet intervention in Afghanistan, but his popularity slumped when he failed to rescue U.S. embassy officials taken as hostages by Iranians. He was heavily defeated in the 1980 election by Ronald Reagan. However, Carter remained active on the international scene, helping to find peaceful solutions to several crises.

Nadia Comaneci
(born 1961)
In training from the age of six, the Romanian gymnast Nadia Comaneci was a world-class competitor by the mid-1970s. At the 1976 Olympics in Montreal, Canada, her tiny, slender, 14-year-old figure and phenomenal performance made her a star. She became the first gymnast to achieve a perfect score of 10 and went on to achieve seven such scores. She shone again at the 1980 Moscow Olympics before retiring in 1984.

Yves Saint Laurent
(1936-2008)
Saint Lauren was an Algerian-born fashion designer who settled in Paris, where he worked for the famous Christian Dior fashion house, becoming its head in 1957. In 1962, he founded his own fashion house, later opening a chain of boutiques (small dress shops) selling ready-to-wear clothes. Saint Laurent's designs were highly influential, notably the pants suits so popular with the new breed of 1970s businesswomen. Perfumes, colognes, men's clothing, and other products also carried the Saint Laurent label.

Anwar Sadat
(1918–1981)
As president of Egypt (1970–1981), Sadat radically changed his country's policies. He ended Egypt's close relations with the Soviet Union and sought the friendship of the United States. He launched the 1973 Yom Kippur War against Israel but later worked to secure a peace treaty under which Egypt recovered the Israeli-occupied Sinai peninsula. Many Arabs were angered by the treaty, and Egypt's severe economic problems also made Sadat unpopular, leading to his assassination in 1981.

Mother Teresa
(1910–1997)
A Roman Catholic nun, Mother Teresa became famous for her work in India, where her hostel in Calcutta (now Kolkata) cared for the old, the sick, and the dying. In 1950, she founded the Order of the Missionaries of Charity, which established hostels in many parts of the world. Much honored in the 1970s, Mother Teresa was awarded the Nobel Prize for Peace in 1979. In 2003, she was beatified (declared blessed) by Pope John Paul II.

Glossary

acumen Shrewdness or intelligence.

autonomy Self-government. A region or country is described as autonomous when it runs its own affairs but is not completely independent. For example, it may be responsible to a central government that keeps control of certain big decisions such as making war or peace.

ballot A vote, or the process of voting.

bazooka A tube-shaped infantry weapon that fires armor-piercing missiles.

CIA The Central Intelligence Agency, the organization that conducts spying, secret information gathering, and similar missions for the U.S. government.

colonial era The period when European states possessed empires, governing peoples on other continents. The British Empire was the largest of the colonial empires.

commando A member of the armed forces who has been trained in special operations skills, for example, night raiding on enemy positions.

communism A political system in which the state owns most property and controls economic activity. In practice, the Soviet Union and other communist states were run exclusively by their Communist Parties.

conclave A secret or private meeting, especially the conclave of cardinals held to elect a new pope.

conservative Opposed to change or believing that changes should be introduced only slowly and cautiously.

contraception The prevention of pregnancy by artificial means.

coup A sudden seizure of power.

Cultural Revolution The campaign launched in 1966 by the Chinese communist leader Mao Zedong. It was intended to revive China's revolutionary spirit but in fact proved oppressive and created chaotic conditions.

democracy A political system in which the citizens elect, and can change, their leaders.

Democrat A member or supporter of the Democrats, one of the two main political parties in the United States.

détente A relaxation of the tensions between states with conflicting aims or ideas.

dictatorship A political system or situation in which a country is ruled by one person or a small group, without the consent of its people.

embargo A government order that forbids citizens to trade with a country regarded as hostile.

fascist A person, party or government that favors a military style dictatorship and values obedience rather than freedom.

guerrillas Fighters who wage hit-and-run warfare, usually against a stronger enemy. They often take advantage of a mountainous or jungle environment in which they can hide.

hijack To seize control illegally of a ship, plane, or vehicle. The intention is usually to hold the passengers as hostages while making political demands, or to transport the hijackers to a particular destination.

inflation Rising prices.

IRA The Irish Republican Army. Until recently, the IRA was an armed group aiming to overthrow the Northern Irish state and unite the region with the Irish Republic.

liberal A word that has many meanings, but generally suggests tolerance, open-mindedness, and willingness to change.

Khmer Rouge The communist movement in Cambodia.

martial law Military law, which is swifter, less fair, and harsher than the ordinary laws under which citizens live. In emergencies, martial law is often declared, replacing the ordinary laws until normality returns.

motorcade A procession of cars, carrying one or more famous or powerful individuals.

National Guard Military reserve units in the United States that can be called into service by either the federal or individual state governments.

nationalize To take a firm or industry into state ownership.

nuclear power plant A power station in which the heat for producing steam to generate electricity is derived from a nuclear reactor (in which controlled nuclear fission takes place).

radical A person or policy favoring fundamental and far reaching change.

recession An economic downturn, often featuring high unemployment, falling production of goods and shrinking markets.

repartee Swift or clever responses made in conversation.

ROTC Reserve Officers' Training Corps, a college-based program that commissions officers for the U.S. armed forces. The program focuses on leadership development, problem solving, strategic planning, and professional ethics.

socialist A person who believes in socialism, a political system in which a country's main industries are owned and run by the state for the general benefit.

Soviet Union A huge state, also known as the USSR. Though often referred to as "Russia," it actually consisted of present-day Russia and a number of other East European, Baltic, and Central Asian countries. The leading communist power, the Soviet Union existed from 1922 to 1991.

Index

Page numbers in **bold** refer to illustrations